(re)collect JONATHAN SHAW

Edited by Debra Klomp

Jonathan dedicates this publication to Nikki and Joshua

Foreword

By Debra Klomp

(re)collect **is published** by Pavilion, in association with Leeds Met Gallery and Coventry University. It has emerged out of the commissioning by Pavilion of Jonathan Shaw, a photographer at a point in his career where craft, concept and aesthetic are melding together in a fascinating and intriguing way. It also reflects a wider partnership with Leeds Met Gallery, which included a solo exhibition of Shaw's work featuring the newly commissioned pieces.

Through the creation of *Victoria Gardens* and *Corn Xchange*, in which he has responded to the city of Leeds and its people, Shaw's work can be seen to be a site of construction, in which the depiction of public space and the public, intersect intriguingly with the mechanics of the act of imaging through the lens. The vision which he creates re-presents our world just as it is, and yet different.

Pavilion's interest in Shaw's work originates from that facet of his practice which embodies the inimitable asset of the photograph—its indexicality, and the manner by which he retains its integrity. Whilst Shaw is not alone in the creation of one negative on an entire length of 120 film, the work of Esteban Pastorino Diaz comes to mind here (as does the large-format school photograph of yesteryear), his methodology of making can be seen to integrate suitably with the chosen subject matter. Once displayed on the gallery wall, this results in an active dialogue between the photographic artifact and the viewer, and it is this which Jean Baird explores in her essay *Revelation, Occlusion and Some Serious Misunderstandings*. Shaw's methodology of construction and aesthetic, is interestingly transferred (or translated) into the new interactive installations, but the binding thread is how they continue to engage the audience in a physical dialogue. In his essay *Playing With Time*, Peter Ride situates this new work within the current trends of other established artists, including Mike Figgis and Sam Taylor-Wood amongst others.

Established in 1983, Pavilion's philosophy is that photography is a medium uniquely placed to inform people's lives and to explore and understand the world in which we live. One of Pavilion's key objectives is the promotion and development of contemporary photographic practice, and to place it firmly within the context of prevalent societal, creative and theoretical debate. Over the course of twenty-two years, the company has successfully achieved this through a sustained delivery of commissions, exhibitions and occasional publications, bringing together social engagement, cutting edge photography and insightful critique. The commissioning of emerging practitioners, at a pivotal point in their evolving careers, is crucial to maintaining this vision.

Jonathan Shaw's exploration of time and motion, in new and innovative ways, not only contributes to our understanding of visual cultures but it also firmly meets Pavilion's key objectives to engage directly with audiences. The *Victoria Gardens* and *Corn Xchange* commissions were a collaboration between photographer, commissioner and the people of Leeds and *(re)collect* showcases this in the context of Shaw's wider practice. Significant financial support was provided by the Esmée Fairbairn Foundation and Arts Council England.

Victoria Gardens, 22nd October 2005, Leeds, UK, 2005, C-type print on Plexiglas, 1.8m x 9m

Victoria Gardens, 22nd October 2005, installed at Leeds Met Gallery, Leeds, UK, 2006

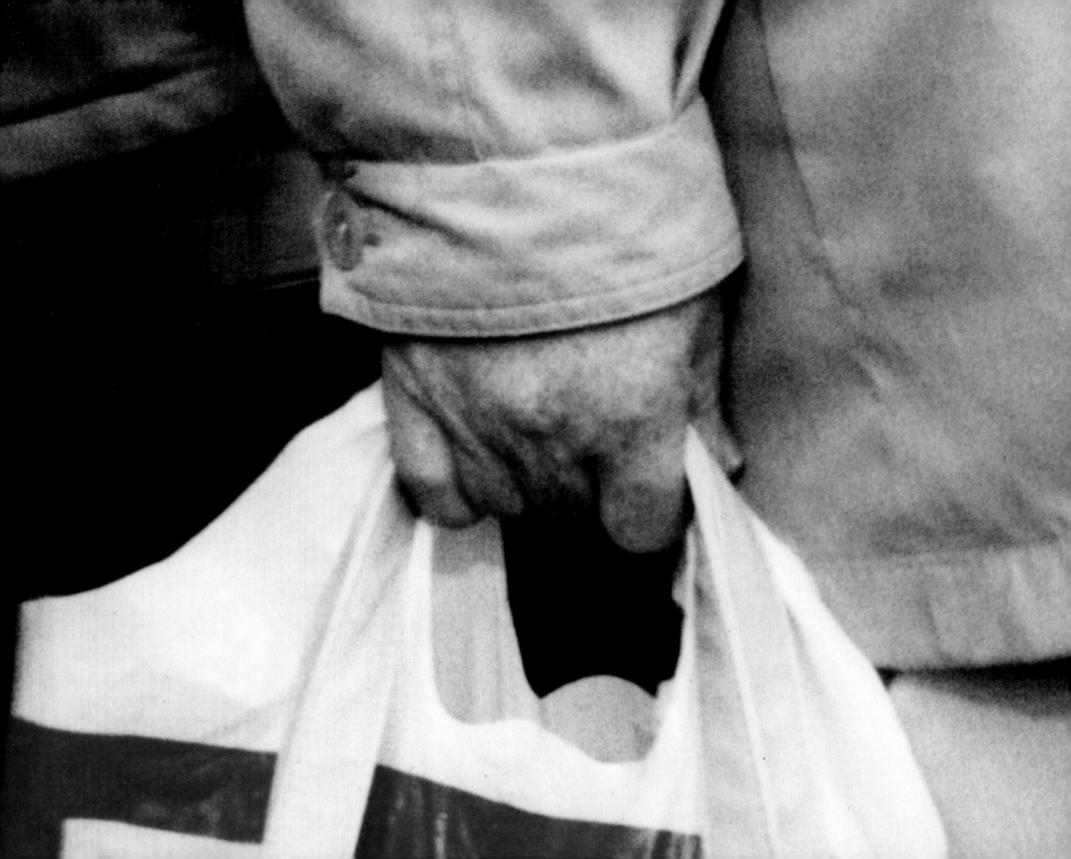

Playing with Time

By Peter Ride

Time has always been a prime concern in photography. Not always as the main subject but always as a collaborative partner. Its role has been key to the way that we have learned to interpret the image.

The 20th Century became the century of the lens, the century in which photography and film became the dominant forms of representation, and also the era of the ubiquitous image. And with this came a language of visualising time and understanding how it is represented, which entered into our visual culture as the norm. The mechanical system of the camera, the interplay of the shutter device with the optics of the lens, made us think of the act of exposure—its timing and duration—as the determining aspect of photography. We learned to read the photograph as being about congruence and juxtaposition, deciphering how the various visual ingredients came together at that exact point in time.

The aesthetic notion of 'the decisive moment' articulated that perfectly as a concern. It taught us that a photograph gave us a moment abstracted from the fluidity of time, and that by inspecting the arrangement of the component parts, this could present us with the opportunity to read huge and complex relationships. Much has been said about the relationship between photography and presumptions of truth and how this has been used, examined and deconstructed; by theorists and artists over the past one hundred and fifty years. But a key aspect in the problematic understanding of what the image does is the psychological affect on the viewer; how we construe the visual material as a form of evidence, how we read subjectivities as objective. Much of this is based upon the understanding that this is 'how things appeared', from a particular point of view, at a particular time and place.

Recently a large number of artists have been playing with time, taking it apart in their images and using the representation of time to present a different quality of experience. Not decrying what has been done before, but finding an approach that builds on our visual vocabulary. This gives an alternative sense of time by acknowledging the power of the fragmented moment, yet placing it within a more complex context.

Jonathan Shaw's body of work places him in a distinguished company of practitioners who are looking at time, as an extended experience in which the point of view of one observer within a single time frame is highly contested. From the *timeslice* photographic work of Tim Macmillan to the video work of Grace Weir and Sam Taylor-Wood, to the multi-narrative cinematic *Timecode* by Mike Figgis, a new range of work is emerging which defies genre, but which always asks questions about the way that experience is relative to different time frames. Often, these artworks not only reflect the complexities for the observer, but they also suggest complexities that operate for the participants whose experiences are relative, not fixed.

Jonathan Shaw's latest work takes a particular approach to this area of interest. In his early images actions were played out across the field of vision. Athletes leaped and dancers spun across the image, leaving the hypnotic trail of physical gestures. On a dance floor, clubbers' bodies twisting and thrusting became a series of extruded movements. In these works the representation of movement was the indicator of time, and the visualisation treated it like molten toffee, stretching it so that it coalesced into strange shapes, some lumpy, some seemingly strained to a point of high tension. But in his more recent work, Jonathan Shaw has moved away from the dramatic gesture, and instead concentrates on the presence of individuals or groups of individuals. In doing so, he engages with the social dynamics within a given space and how people are identifying with each other and with that space. His subjects appear much less to be taking over space, running through time, instead they are navigating their way through

Making of **Corn Xchange** and **Victoria Gardens** in Leeds, UK

smaller moments. They occupy a gentler, more intimate space.

Jonathan Shaw has evolved both the mechanics of his operation and the creative approach to achieve this. He uses, as he had previously, a modified TLR camera in which the film is moving across the shutter plane at a constant speed for the duration of the shot, but the camera motion is now enabled by a tracking system, like a dolly used in cine photography, rather than handheld. This gives a continuous steady motion, but it also means that the speed of his movement can be in direct correlation to the distance he aims to cover and the length of the final image. For *Victoria Gardens* (2005), this results in a single negative that measures 310mm, exactly corresponding to the twenty-five seconds duration of his shot. The resulting print is nine metres in length, exactly the length of the space he traversed in Victoria Gardens. Therefore the viewer, when passing in front of the print on the gallery wall to view it, takes the same journey that Jonathan had done.

Jonathan Shaw's creative approach has also moved from a documentary point of view to a participatory one. The participants in *Victoria Gardens* are all people, who in the previous weeks he had observed in the square, which is a significant pedestrian thoroughfare and meeting place in the centre of Leeds. Inviting them back to the space where he had first seen them, he has facilitated a re-enactment of several encounters and small moments: friends meeting, people passing through, workers taking their break and a couple about to get married. The result is part performance, part tableaux vivant. The different clusters of people, each with their own sense of focus are unrelated to each other and yet linked to each other in the same space. Jonathan Shaw's technique lifts them from their background, abstracting them from the appearance of an overall, masterly, point of view. In the same way that when a passenger on a moving train focuses on an object in the foreground, the background becomes the moving blur—or vice versa, the participants from the viewers' point of view are crisp against a strangely Plastacene background. Still figures caught in the swirl of time.

This results in a subtler, more quizzical relationship with time, than in earlier images. It reflects not only the time taken for the moment of observation, but also the way that our cognitive processes works across that time, selectively drawing on different moments and occurrences and then moving on. It reflects the often held argument in photography, that we are never impartial observers but instead highly selective viewers.

The power of traditional photography can be said to lie in the fact that it shows us things as we do not see them, since we do not experience time in split seconds, but instead experience the fluidity of time. Jonathan Shaw's work brings home how complicated our visual perception is, how we are making visual choices that construct meaning across time.

Corn Xchange, Leeds, UK, 2006, Digital Video Installation, 11m 22s, selected video stills

Indecisive Moments

By Debra Klomp

Shaw's photographic work occupies a tenuous space between the moving and the still image. This is an asset in his work which ensures the images are anything but passive and demand an active scopic and physical relationship with the viewer. Reading them is not meant to be easily resolved.

His exploration of time through interactive video is equally arresting and self-assured. In the large-scale photographs, subjects remain in focus by maintaining a static position during the act of being imaged. In Shaw's new interactive work (*Doncaster* and *Corn Xchange*), however, the opposite occurs. Subjects must physically remain in shot, following the video camera as it rotates, capturing images at three frames per second and independent of Shaw. Shaw might also be seen to relinquish control of what is imaged; he leaves the camera to 'shoot', unattended in

a perspex box. But this observation is far from the reality. For another key shift in Shaw's new work, is a re-negotiated dialogue with the subject/spectator.

Several hours of moving image is edited into a seamless loop of approximately 15 minutes and, unlike the photographs (which are constructed live), the construction happens in the editing suite. Further, a direct intervention is invited from the viewer, who is able to control the speed and direction of the final projected piece—thus the gallery attendee emerges as spectator and controller simultaneously, by being able to speed up, slow down, reverse and fast forward.

Beside the rhythm and aesthetic quality of Shaw's work, which binds together the still and moving image, it is his relationship with the subject and/or viewer which is most intriguing and anything but passive.

Frenchgate Centre, installed in Doncaster, UK, 2004, Digital Video Installation, 14m 32s

Frenchgate Centre, selected video stills

Making of and installing **Gallery 13, 10th August 2002** at Birmingham Museum & Art Gallery 2003, Birmingham, UK

Gallery 13, 10th August 2002, installed at Birmingham Museum & Art Gallery, Birmingham, UK, 2003, C-type print on PVC, 1.25m x 13.5m

Top Tips
to Beat Boredom

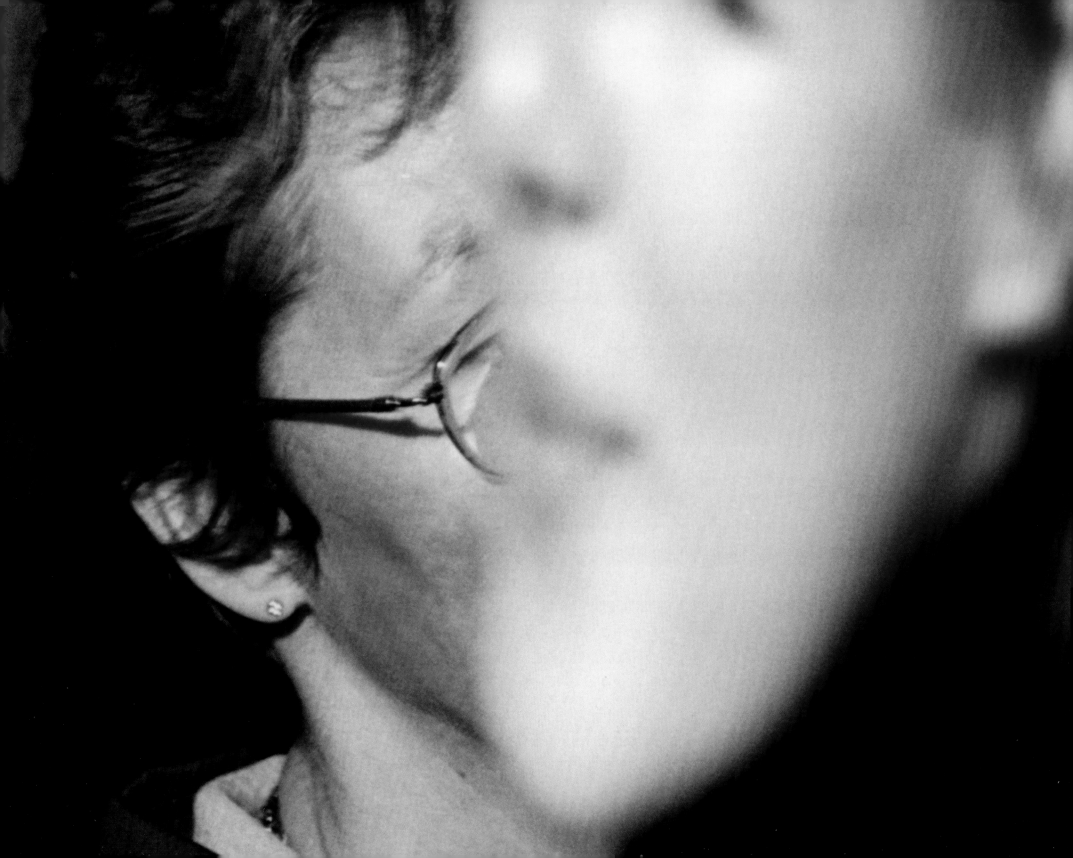

Crash 7, London, UK, 2001 (continued overleaf)

Crash 7, installed at Leeds Met Gallery, Leeds, UK, 2006, photographic print on polyester, 2.5m x 4.6m

Revelation, Occlusion and Some Serious Misunderstandings

By Jean Baird

On November 26th 1881 a photographer, a scientist and a few select others assemble in Paris at E.J. Marey's house on the Boulevard Delessert. A confluence of art and science — these men are here because of their various attempts to discover and depict the true condition of nature. Marey is captivated by a series of extraordinary visual revelations that are the result of innovations in photographic technology, pioneered by Eadward Muybridge and demonstrated through his zoopraxiscope, a device which projects painted images taken from photographs across a screen. Muybridge's photographs, each of which records a single instance of a particular gait of the horse, unfurl sequential moments and movements that are, subsequently, magically reanimated to reveal and represent the truth about the horse's motion. Knowledge, illusion, science, art coalesce into a convoluted narrative of revelation and occlusion.

Marey has seen Muybridge's photographic sequences of Stanford's horse, Occident, that prove that all four feet leave the ground during a gallop. Leland Stanford, railway magnate and Governor of California, had engaged the photographer to supply visual proof of the horse's gait. The commissioning of Muybridge originated from Stanford's knowledge of Marey's experiments (1873) with a device called the pneumatic shoe. Etienne-Jules Marey, a scientist-physiologist, innovator and inventor, had listened to the sound and deciphered the trace of the footfall of the horse. Muybridge's photographs support Marey's observations; Marey is excited by the idea of using 'a chemical sensor' as he believes human senses are unreliable and apt to deceive. One had to "invent processes of direct inscription, so as to separate life from its secrets, put it in the open and force a direct writing from it". Marey has already experimented with photography, but Muybridge's innovations meant that there was now the opportunity for a writing of life, that would also picture what was beyond the capacity of human vision.

Motion is spasmodic; it is the result of phases of acceleration, stuttering stops and starts and Muybridge's photographic apparatus does not provide an accurate or adaptable enough visual record of time and motion for the purposes of the newly emerging science of physiology. For Marey, the meeting with Muybridge is not an unqualified success, and when he leaves Paris shortly afterwards he is already conceiving of a camera that will record motion in successive phases from one point of view, improving his inventions until he finally produces the apparatus in 1892, that makes the invention of cinema possible. The scientific, if not artistic, interest in Muybridge's project evaporates.

Marey uses movement against movement, one known against another one under investigation. By the use of rotating discs with slits that act as shutters, he knows the time taken between each figure recorded by the film. This is a system that freezes motion at regular, measurable intervals, distributing successive images over the surface of one piece of film in a fixed plate camera. There are other cameras that record continuously onto moving film, where the subject is draped in black against a dark background so that all that remains visible are white lines, dots and points which mark the skeleton or limbs. The outline of the moving body is lost in a dark anamorphosis, but bones and limbs form lines that trace, write and graph phases of motion. In Chronophotography, technical innovation results in pictorial metamorphosis as the picture, as a comprehensible and coherent unity of time and space, as a perspectival system of representation, a decisive moment, is undone. Chronophotographs are pictures where a trace is also writing, photographs that write time before light.

Muybridge's work captures phases of motion arbitrarily divided into sections, and time is a consequence of reading horizontally and vertically along the sequence of images.

Work installed at Goethe Institute, Dresden, Germany, 2005 and the Birmingham Museum & Art Gallery, UK, 2003

While his photographic tableau preserves the conventional coherency of the picture space, the sequences are not always constructed out of consecutive images; there are gaps and occlusions, differences in cropping, repeated images and even empty frames. Despite the inconsistencies of form, we recognise something familiar in this pictorial representation of time and motion. Closer to art than science they create a fantasy of movement through narration and suggestion in the idiom of photographic realism, played out through the revelation of bodies crossing and overlapping over and upon the space of the screen. Muybridge's tableau are epitomised as a technological way of seeing, normalised and objectified through an apparent 'scientificity', borrowed from its propinquity to Marey's less well-known and less well-understood work. "It is as if", says Hollis Frampton, "that the photograph could no longer contain the contradictory pressure to affirm time and deny it. It split

sharply into an illusionist cinema of incessant motion and a static photographic art that remained frozen solid for decades". He continues, "There are two different sorts of perceptual time. I propose to call one historic and the other ecstatic."

Like Etienne-Jules Marey before him, Jonathan Shaw uses movement against movement to make either the moving or stationary subject appear or disappear. What he photographs is modified by the choreography of the movement of his own body, or the organisation of a scene that is not unlike the activity of Muybridge. Shaw does not measure or objectify what is in front of his lens, he is paying attention to the activity of his subjects, their way of being, an existence in time that is not separate from his own. The interchange between scene and seen is vitally important; Shaw is interested in the visual as it is organised as a form of spectacle. This is evident in the pictures of theatre or sport, but the other pictures are also spectacles; they

take place where the architecture of the street orders the activity of people into particular relations with that locale, with each other, relations modified by the self-consciousness of looking and being looked at in public and mediated in relation to the camera.

Despite the hundred years between Shaw, Muybridge and Marey, and despite the digital displacement of the indexical trace of light on film, there remains a stubborn belief in the photograph as evidence of a truth secured precisely through the capture of historic time, the truth and knowledge of nature that Marey sought to find in the unseen interstices of the visual. In Shaw's photographs everything is relentlessly surveyed by a modified shutter that builds the picture up out of thin strips of sight, like a photo-finish camera that moves with the winning horse right across the racecourse. Technical innovation results in pictorial metamorphosis, which results in a photographic vision true to life and true to motion as everything that lives, moves.

What Jonathan Shaw's photographs reveal in their panoramic sweep is a photographic time at once both historic and ecstatic, where the ecstasy of subjective perception becomes a social phenomenon caught in the mingling of perceptual time. They show us a time that moves at a different pace in the same place, relative to its orchestration by the artist and the location. We are not held captive by these images and cannot view them from a stationary perspective. Shaw's subjects look back at us; they participate in our observation as they give themselves to be seen by the camera, only there is no certainty that they will appear, as only things that are placed at the point of focus of the lens reassemble in the image in proportion to their real forms. The exchange of the gaze between subject/photographer/camera/spectator is grounded precisely in this uncertainty of the photographic trace, which restores the wildness and wonder of the truly photographic in an era dedicated to it's digital simulation.

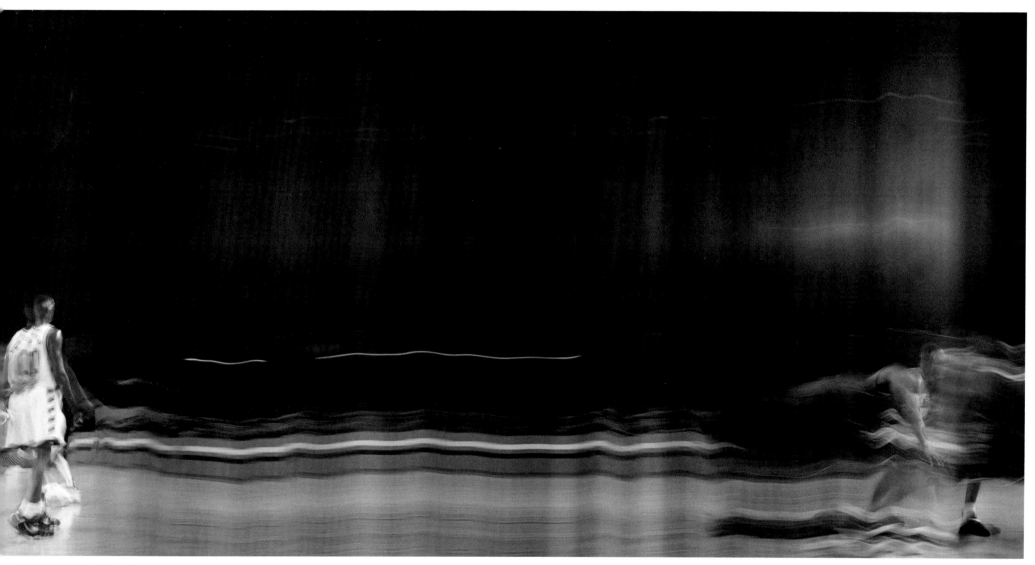

Basketball (detail), London Towers versus Manchester Giants, Budweiser Basketball Championships, Wembley Arena, London, UK, 1996, C-type print on aluminium, 45cm x 2.5m

Edward II (Blue) (detail), Birmingham Royal Ballet, Birmingham Hippodrome, Birmingham, UK, 1997, C-type print on aluminium, 30cm x 2.5m

New Street (detail), Birmingham, UK, 1997, C-type print on aluminium, 24cm x 3m

New Street (detail), Birmingham, UK, 1997, C-type print on aluminium, 24cm x 3m

Biographical Information

Peter Ride

Peter Ride is Co-Director and Senior Research Fellow at the Centre for Arts Research Technology and Education (CARTE), University of Westminster and Artistic Director of DA2, Digital Arts Development Agency. DA2 is an organisation that devises, commissions and produces new media arts projects. Other work includes interdisciplinary research projects at the University of Westminster. He was one of the first curators in the UK to work on internet and digitally networked arts projects. Previously Peter Ride was the Arts Programme co-ordinator for Artec, the Arts Technology Centre, London (1995–1997) and the Director of Cambridge Darkroom Gallery (1992–1995). Publications include *The New Media Handbook* (Routledge, 2006), co-authored with Andrew Dewdney.

Jean Baird

Jean Baird is Senior Lecturer in the Theory and Practice of Photography at Nottingham Trent University. As an Artist and writer, Jean Baird's recent research projects include AVP (Audio-Visual-Performance), working as one of a group of artists establishing an interdisciplinary and collaborative practice concerned with 'extended technologies', working with image, experimental improved music, and text. Interest in Jonathan Shaw's work comes from the research project *Magic! Writing and Transformation in Photography*. Jean Baird was part of the show *Magic Within Reason* (May, 2004) at Domo Baal, London. This research investigates the experience of photography as 'magical', from it's roots in the 19th Century to date. Jean Baird has moved to Nottingham Trent University via Glasgow School of Art and Derby University, having worked in both England and the United States.

Debra Klomp

Debra Klomp is the Director of Pavilion, curating its programme, editing its publications and responsible for the overall strategic management of the company. Previously she was a lecturer in Photographic Practice at Coventry University (1991–1995) and Historical and Theoretical Studies at Derby University (1996), Media Officer at Arts Council England (1998–2003) and Administrator at Seeing The Light (1995–1998). As a practitioner she was a founding member of the 'Positive Image' photographic group in Coventry (UK). Debra Klomp's work has appeared in publications including *Nexus Vol. 5 – Face to Face: Directions in Contemporary Women's Portraiture* (Scarlet Press, 1998), is represented by IRIS – International Centre of Women in Photography and is also a freelance curator of contemporary photography.

Jonathan Shaw

Jonathan Shaw studied photography, graphic design and computer graphics at the University of the West of England between 1990 and 1996, and completed his Masters at the University of Central England in 1997. During this time he developed a fascination with the conceptual, theoretical and mechanical relationships which exist between time, movement and the still image. He is currently Senior Lecturer, Lens Based Media within the School of Art & Design at Coventry University.

Solo Exhibitions

2006 *(re)collect,* Leeds Met Gallery, Leeds (UK)

1998 *Kinematographs – Representations of Time, Movement and the Still Image,* F-Stop Media Station, Bath (UK)

Group Exhibitions

2005 Geothe Institute, Dresden (Germany)

2005 *Time/Place/Presence,* Lanchester Gallery, Coventry (UK)

2004 *Eadweard Muybridge: moving on,* Penny School Gallery, Kingston upon Thames (UK)

2004 D-Frost Festival, Doncaster (UK)

2003 *Time/Motion* – Photographs by E. Muybridge, H. Edgerton & J. Shaw, Birmingham Museum and Art Gallery, Birmingham (UK)

2003 Artlounge, Birmingham (UK)

2002 *Homegrown,* Chuck Works, Birmingham (UK)

2001 Rotunda One Five, Birmingham (UK)

2001 *Something Old, Something New,* Birmingham Museum and Art Gallery, Birmingham (UK)

2000 *Cultivate,* Orange Studio, Birmingham (UK)

2000 Showcased *Bytesized* digital commission, Radiator Digital Festival, Nottingham (UK)

2000 Showcased *Bytesized* digital commission, Lovebytes Digital Festival, Sheffield (UK)

2000 *West Midlands Photography Portfolio Showcase,* Midlands Arts Centre, Birmingham (UK)

1999 *Revolution* (Forward Festival), International Convention Centre, Birmingham (UK)

1999 *About Time* (The International Festival of Contemporary Time Based Arts), Howard Gardens Gallery, Cardiff (UK)

1998 *New Designers,* Business Design Centre, London (UK)

1997 *The Big Peg*, Birmingham (UK)

Commissions

2005 Pavilion, Leeds (UK)

2005 NHS, Birmingham and Black Country (UK)

2004 D-Frost Festival, Doncaster (UK)

2003 Birmingham Museum & Art Gallery, Birmingham (UK)

2002 Manhattan Loft Corporation, London (UK)

2002 City of Culture Campaign, Birmingham (UK)

2001 Branson Coates Architecture, London (UK)

2000 Volkswagen (UK)

1999 Forward Festival, Birmingham City Council, Birmingham (UK)

1999 Vivid, Birmingham (UK)

1999 Citigate Dewe Rogerson, Birmingham (UK)

Collections

Arts Council of England, West Midlands (UK)

Birmingham Central Library Photography Archives (UK)

Birmingham Museum & Art Gallery (UK)

Awards

2003 Shortlisted for Paul Hamlyn Award

2002 Creative Ambitions Award, Arts Council of England

1999 Photography Portfolio Award, Arts Council of England

Publications

2006 *(re)collect* – Jonathan Shaw, published by Pavilion (UK)

2003 *Time/Motion* – E. Muybridge, H. Edgerton & J. Shaw, Dewi Lewis Publishing

2003 *Guide to Ecstacity* – Nigel Coates, Laurence King Publishing

2003 *Bull Ring the Heart of Birmingham*, Michael Hallett

2003 *100 Habits of Successful Graphic Designers*, Plazm

Acknowledgements

Pavilion and Jonathan Shaw would like to thank all who participated in the main shoot of *Victoria Gardens* in October 2005 and the making of *Corn Xchange*.

Pavilion, Leeds Met Gallery and Jonathan Shaw would also like to thank the following individuals for their valuable contribution, support and insight toward the *(re)collect* exhibition and catalogue.

Pavilion Team: Angela Frost, Ruth Haycock, Jamie Hutchison, Debra Klomp.

Leeds Met Gallery Team: Andy Abbott, Moira Innes, Jaye Kearney, Andi Noble, Paul Noble, Dave Ronalds, Debbie Shadwell, Jon Slight, Katy Woods.

Volunteer Assistants on the Victoria Gardens *and* Corn Xchange *Commissions:*
Lesley Calderwood, Lynsey Grace, Rachel Harkin, Minna Marfo, Nicola McAteer, Rebecca Rowley and Chris Staff.

Additionally: Nikki, Margaret and Christopher Shaw, Mildred Sowden, Max Kandhola (Pavilion Board of Trustees), Peter James (Birmingham Central Library), Jane Arthur and Reyahn King (Birmingham Museum and Art Gallery), Emma Cheshire and Nick Slater (Arts Council England), Andy Smith (AAJ Engineers), Paul Mullen and Team (Panik Technology), Eva, Steve Jones and Simon Gahan (Palm Laboratories), Lisa Thadderton (The Corn Exchange), Simon Peel and David Fraser, Darren Ching, Peter Ride, Jean Baird and Coventry School of Art and Design.

Published in 2006 by Pavilion
Pavilion, Host Media Centre,
21 Savile Mount,
Leeds LS7 3HZ
+44 (0) 113 200 7061
www.pavilion.org.uk

In association with Coventry University
and Leeds Met Gallery.

Copyright © 2006
For the photographs: Jonathan Shaw
For the installation photographs:
John Spinks (p. 24, 25, 37), Peter James (p. 23),
Dave Reemes (p. 36, 37), Lynsey Grace (p. 15),
Nicola McAteer (p. 14)

For the texts: Jean Baird, Peter Ride, Debra Klomp
For this edition: Pavilion

ISBN: 0-9544775-2-9

Published in an edition of 1,000

Cover Image: *New Street*, Birmingham, UK, 1997
by Jonathan Shaw

Designed by Darren Ching, New York (USA)
Edited by Debra Klomp, Pavilion (UK)
Printed by EBS, Verona (Italy)

Distribution by Pavilion